Incredible Plants!

Why We Need Plants

Josh Gregory

Children's Press®
An Imprint of Scholastic Inc.

Content Consultant
Michael Freeling, PhD
Professor
Department of Plant & Microbial Biology
University of California, Berkeley
Berkeley, California

Library of Congress Cataloging-in-Publication Data
Names: Gregory, Josh, author.
Title: Why We Need Plants / by Josh Gregory.
Description: New York, NY : Children's Press, an imprint of Scholastic Inc., 2020. | Series: A true book |
 Includes bibliographical references and index.
Identifiers: LCCN 2019004807| ISBN 9780531234662 (library binding) | ISBN 9780531240090
 (paperback)
Subjects: LCSH: Human-plant relationships—History—Juvenile literature. | Plants and civilization—
 Juvenile literature.
Classification: LCC QK46.5.H85 G74 2020 | DDC 581.6/3—dc23
LC record available at https://lccn.loc.gov/2019004807

All rights reserved. Published in 2020 by Children's Press, an imprint of Scholastic Inc.
Printed in Heshan, China 62

SCHOLASTIC, CHILDREN'S PRESS, A TRUE BOOK™, and associated logos are trademarks and/or registered trademarks of Scholastic Inc.

Scholastic Inc., 557 Broadway, New York, NY 10012

1 2 3 4 5 6 7 8 9 10 R 29 28 27 26 25 24 23 22 21 20

Front cover: A child holding carrots
Back cover: Deforestation in the Amazon

Find the Truth!

Everything you are about to read is true *except* for one of the sentences on this page.

Which one is **TRUE**?

T or F People need plants to survive.

T or F The first genetically modified plants were produced in 2010.

Find the answers in this book.

Contents

The **BIG** Truth

GMOs: A Big Debate

"GMO" stands for
genetically modified
organism.

GENETICALLY
GMO
MODIFIED

4

Cauliflower

A young gardener

Think About It!

Take a look at this photo. What do you think is happening? It looks like someone is growing lettuce. But what are those red lights? Where are the soil and tractors? At this factory near Tokyo, Japan, workers can grow lettuce three to four times faster than on a farm. Red LED bulbs are used in place of sunlight, and the plants have the perfect amount of soil and water.

Intrigued?
Want to know more? Turn the page!

A scientist studies soybean plants that are part of an experiment.

Factory-grown lettuce is just one of the latest results of humans interacting with the plant **kingdom**. Throughout history, we have shared an inseparable bond with plants. Plants create the oxygen we breathe. They feed us, and we use them to make everything from clothes to medicine. At the same time, people have had a major impact on plants. Some of these effects have been harmful, from damaging plant habitats to causing plant **species** to disappear completely.

There are hundreds of thousands of known plant species living today. And new ones are discovered all the time. Plants are found all over the world, in habitats ranging from ocean waters to rocky mountaintops. Depending on where you go, the plants can look very different, from towering trees to tiny flowers. But in almost every environment, plants and people have a very close relationship.

Many people grow gardens of flowers or food.

The earliest hunter-gatherer societies formed about 2 million years ago.

As their name says, hunter-gatherers relied on animals they could hunt and plants they could gather for food.

Planting Seeds in the Soil

Early human societies were based around hunting and gathering. People did not yet know how to grow their own plants. Instead, they collected fruits, nuts, and other foods from wild plants. People's diets varied depending on where they were living and what season it was. They had to move around often in search of food. This type of **nomadic** life could support only small communities.

Ancient Egyptians timed the planting of their crops to take advantage of the Nile River's regular flooding.

Settling Down

The development of agriculture was a major turning point in human history. About 12,000 years ago, people in the Middle East began planting seeds to grow crops such as peas and lentils. Farming provided a more reliable source of food than gathering did, and people were able to settle down. They built towns, and populations grew. They also had more time to spend learning new skills and creating technology, including improved tools for farming.

New Ways to Grow

One important agricultural improvement in the 6000s BCE was **irrigation**. This process transports water to drier places. The first farms had to be close to bodies of water or in areas with plenty of rain. But with irrigation, people could farm in new locations.

Greenhouses were another improvement. They helped farmers grow plants in different climates. Though similar buildings have existed since about 30 CE, the first modern greenhouses were created in the 1800s.

Greenhouses let in the sun's energy without exposing plants to the wind, cold, and other weather outside.

Creating Better Crops

As people learned more about how and why plants grow, they found ways to change the plants themselves. For thousands of years, farmers have understood that plants can be bred to have certain qualities. A farmer might want to raise especially large tomatoes. Each year, the farmer chooses the plants that produce the biggest fruit and breeds them together. Over time, this results in a crop that produces only large tomatoes.

Timeline of Agricultural Advancements

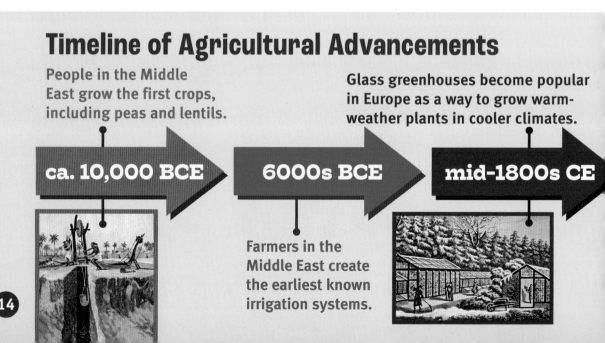

People in the Middle East grow the first crops, including peas and lentils.

ca. 10,000 BCE

Farmers in the Middle East create the earliest known irrigation systems.

6000s BCE

Glass greenhouses become popular in Europe as a way to grow warm-weather plants in cooler climates.

mid-1800s CE

In the 1800s, scientists such as Gregor Mendel learned how plants and animals get traits from their parents. This knowledge helped scientists breed plants with specific qualities more easily. They even bred different plants together to create new **hybrid** species. Today's sweet corn is a combination of multiple corn types. Grapefruits are a hybrid of oranges and pomelos. Other plant varieties were created to resist diseases or grow more easily in certain climates.

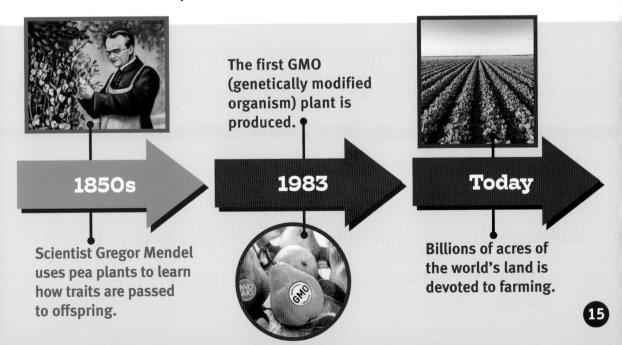

The first GMO (genetically modified organism) plant is produced.

1850s

1983

Today

Scientist Gregor Mendel uses pea plants to learn how traits are passed to offspring.

Billions of acres of the world's land is devoted to farming.

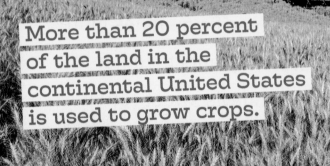

More than 20 percent of the land in the continental United States is used to grow crops.

Sprawling modern farms would not be possible without help from machines such as combines. Combines simplify the process of harvesting grain.

A World Full of Farms

Farming is just as important today as it was to the earliest civilizations. With more than 7.5 billion humans on earth, we need to produce a lot of plants to maintain our lifestyle. More than 2 billion acres (809 million ha) of land around the world is used for growing crops. In comparison, the entire United States covers about 2.3 billion acres (931 million ha)!

Growing at Home

Not all plants are grown on huge farms. People around the world grow plants at home. Some growers do it to provide fresh fruits, vegetables, and herbs for their families. In the United States alone, more than one-third of all households grow food in private gardens. Other gardeners simply want to make their yards look nice. They carefully arrange colorful flowers and shady trees. Many people find gardening to be a relaxing and rewarding hobby.

Gardens can provide beauty and food.

17

Floating markets in Thailand sell fruits, vegetables, flowers, and other goods from boats.

People who don't eat foods that come from animal products, such as meat and dairy, are called vegans.

Plants on Our Plates

Plants contain many important **nutrients** that our bodies need. Many nutrients, such as vitamin C and dietary fiber, are difficult or impossible to get without eating plants. Plant foods are also cheaper and easier to produce than meat or dairy. As a result, humans have long relied on plants as the main source of nutrition in their diets. All around the world, people have found countless tasty ways to prepare and enjoy plants as food.

Fresh Flavors

When you visit a market or grocery store, you will see an incredible range of plant parts on display. Colorful fruits come in all shapes and sizes. There are also leafy greens, herbs, and piles of grains, nuts, and beans. Even the roots of many plants are edible. On the next page are just a few examples of fresh, whole plant foods that many people eat all the time.

A single meal might contain leaves, stems, seeds, fruit, and other plant parts.

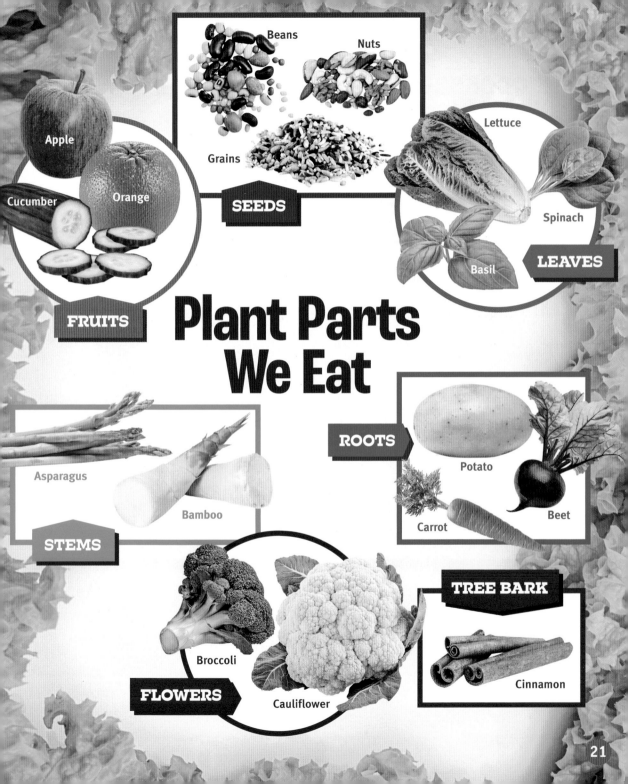

Plant Parts We Eat

Beans

Nuts

Grains

SEEDS

Apple

Cucumber

Orange

FRUITS

Lettuce

Spinach

Basil

LEAVES

Asparagus

Bamboo

STEMS

ROOTS

Potato

Carrot

Beet

Broccoli

Cauliflower

FLOWERS

TREE BARK

Cinnamon

Processed Plants

Plants are also ingredients in some foods that might surprise you. For example, mustard probably doesn't look like any plant part you've seen before. But this tasty topping gets its unique flavor from the seeds of mustard plants. Candy is sweetened with sugar from sugarcane plants or syrup made from corn. Bread and other baked goods are made using flour, which is created by grinding up wheat or other grains.

Mustard seeds are ground down and mixed with other ingredients to create mustard.

Even the meat people eat, such as beef, exists because of plants.

Fuel for Animals

Even meat and dairy products would not exist without plants. Cows, pigs, and chickens all have plants as at least part of their diets. On farms, some livestock might eat corn or potatoes. Other farm animals are able to eat plants that humans cannot digest, such as grass and hay. Cows have special bacteria and multiple stomachs that make it easier to break these plants down and use their nutrients.

GMOs: A Big Debate

GMO stands for "genetically modified organism." Scientists create GMOs by taking **genes** from one species and placing them into the seeds of another. This creates plants with specific qualities.
Some people think GMOs are the future of farming.
Others think GMO plants are harmful. What do you think?

In favor of GMOs

✔ Many scientists agree that GMO foods are safe to eat.

✔ GMO plants can be made to grow better in poor weather or fend off insects. This helps farmers produce more food, which cuts down on food shortages and keeps prices low.

✔ Some foods can be made more nutritious or to stay fresh longer.

✔ Foods can be given special traits. For example, genes from a fish that lives in cold water might make a plant species better at surviving frosty nights.

✔ Some GMO crops produce natural pesticides that drive away insects. This keeps the insects from damaging the crops, and farmers will spray fewer anti-insect pesticides.

Against GMOs

✔ GMO foods may have bad health effects that haven't been discovered yet.

✔ Farmers cannot reuse seeds from many GMO crops that they grow. As a result, farmers need to buy new GMO seeds every year from the companies that make them.

✔ Some GMO crops are created to resist damage from pesticides that kill weeds. But over time, the weeds develop resistance to the same chemicals. As a result, farmers are using more and more anti-weed pesticides.

✔ Some experts fear that GMO plants will breed with wild plants, creating weeds that are difficult to kill. These weeds could overtake natural species, reducing natural **biodiversity**. And once released into the environment, it could be difficult or impossible to remove them.

What do you think?

A backpacker crosses a suspension bridge in a rain forest.

Plants get their green color from a substance called chlorophyll, which is used in photosynthesis.

Plants for Every Purpose

Plants are much more than a source of food and beauty. Through the process of **photosynthesis**, their green leaves create oxygen. This means there is plenty of healthy air for us and all animals on earth to breathe.

Plants are also used to make some of our everyday products, from toilet paper to fuel for cars. You might even be surprised to learn of some household items that come from plants!

Huge factories spin cotton fiber into cloth.

Cotton plant

Plants You Can Wear

Would you wear a plant? Believe it or not, you probably do. Plants are a common source for clothing materials. The most widely used plant is cotton. Cotton plants produce bundles of fluffy, white fiber to protect their seeds. People spin cotton fibers to create thread, which is woven into cloth. The cloth is made into everything from T-shirts and jeans to sweaters and sneakers. Other plant-based textiles include linen, which comes from flax, and hemp, from cannabis.

The Wonders of Wood

People have long used wood to build just about anything you can imagine. Tools, boats, houses, and furniture are examples. This sturdy material comes from the roots, trunks, and branches of trees. Today, trees harvested for their wood are often grown on huge farms.

Wood is also used to make paper. The wood is ground up and mixed with water and chemicals to make wet, soupy pulp. The pulp is then flattened and dried in thin sheets.

This factory turns trees into pulp, which the company sells to other manufacturers to use in products.

Feeling Better

Every plant species contains a huge variety of chemicals to help it thrive in nature. Some of these chemicals can help humans. Long ago, plants were the only medicines people had. Different cultures around the world created medicinal teas, pastes, and other treatments from local plants. Examples include ginseng, cinnamon, and garlic. People weren't sure exactly why certain plants helped treat illness, but they knew the medicines worked.

People drink certain teas to help them feel better when they are sick.

A researcher checks on cassava plants growing in a lab in Côte d'Ivoire.

As people learned more about chemistry and biology, they studied medicinal plants to see why they worked. This led scientists to identify many of the specific chemicals in plants that are beneficial. Scientists can then use the chemicals to make even better medications. This is how aspirin was discovered, for example. It's based on a chemical found in willow tree bark. Plants have helped scientists create painkillers, heart medications, and other important treatments.

Running Clean & Green

On 100% bioDiesel, made by recycling our cooking oil.

wetherspoon caring for the environment

As researchers improve biofuels and they become easier to buy, more vehicles are using them.

Fueled by Plants

Plants have been an important source of fuel for much of human history. Early people relied on wood to fuel fires for warmth and cooking. Today, there are even more ways to use plants as fuel. For example, biodiesel is a kind of biofuel produced from the oil of corn, soybeans, or other plants. It powers cars, airplanes, and other vehicles. It can also heat buildings.

Nature's Colors

Plants are useful for countless other purposes. The indigo plant's leaves are an important ingredient in the rich, purple-blue dye we use for blue jeans. Latex, a milky white substance produced by some plants, is used to make rubber. The leaves of certain palm trees and other plants produce a wax that is in everything from shoe polish to lipstick. The number of things we can make from plants is truly amazing!

People around the world have used indigo dye for thousands of years.

Nearly 2 million acres (809,000 ha) of land burned in California in 2018. That's about the size of Delaware.

Firefighters work to control a wildfire raging in California in 2018.

Disappearing Plants

Not every interaction between people and plants is positive. For example, burning **fossil fuels** such as oil or coal releases chemicals and soot into the atmosphere. This helps cause global climate change. One effect of climate change is that huge wildfires are becoming more common. Such fires can cause tremendous damage to plant populations. Human activities have even led to many plant species becoming endangered or completely extinct.

Plants and Pollution

Plants need healthy air, water, and soil to grow and reproduce. But many common human activities pollute all three resources. Gas-powered cars release chemicals into the air as they burn oil for energy. Harmful waste products from factories can seep into water supplies. Pesticides and other chemicals used to grow plants can damage the soil. All of these things make it harder for wild plants to survive.

Some factories add harmful chemicals into the air, water, and soil.

Some scientists are working on GMO plants that can help remove dangerous pollution from indoor air.

The Future of Forests

The Amazon in South America is the world's largest rain forest. It is home to about 40,000 plant species. Many of these grow nowhere else on earth. But like many forests, the

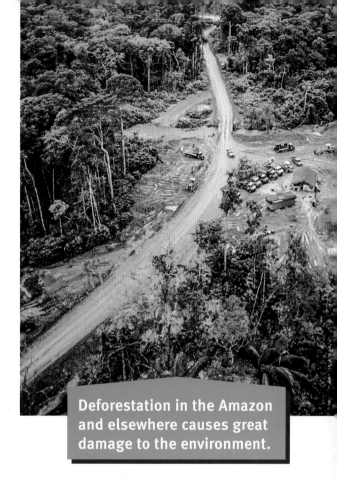

Deforestation in the Amazon and elsewhere causes great damage to the environment.

Amazon is disappearing. Since the 1970s, people have cleared about 20 percent of the Amazon. Most of the cleared land is used for cattle farms. In other places around the world, people are also cutting forests and destroying plants to make room for farms, homes, and businesses.

A Connected World

Human activities also affect wild animals, which in turn impact plants. The populations of several bee species are declining in areas around the world. Flowers and fruit trees rely on bees and other insects to reproduce. Scientists fear these plants could die out as bees disappear.

In addition, harm to plant species can affect animals. If humans clear a forest, many animals lose food sources or even their homes.

Filling a yard or garden with native plants can help provide food and shelter to local birds.

Bird species, including bald eagles, often use trees to build nests where they take care of their young.

Plant Careers

Do you love plants? Here are a few careers where you could work with plants:

Farmers grow and harvest crops of all kinds, whether on small family farms or sprawling plantations.

Botanists are plant scientists. They might study plant genetics or find new uses for plants.

Arborists are sometimes called tree surgeons. Their job includes trimming trees without harming them and diagnosing trees' illnesses.

Landscape architects design beautiful outdoor arrangements of flowers, trees, and other plants.

Gardeners care for plants on the grounds of homes or businesses.

Florists arrange cut flowers to create beautiful designs, from Valentine's Day bouquets to wedding arrangements.

The Svalbard Global Seed Vault is built into permanently frozen ground.

Seeds are kept in plastic containers.

Seed Storage

Many plant experts work to make sure plant species don't disappear, even if they go extinct in the wild. Seed banks store the seeds of many plant varieties for future use. These seeds can be used to reproduce disappearing species or create new GMOs or crossbred species.

The Svalbard Global Seed Vault in Norway protects seeds from all around the world. Samples are kept in a special vault built into the ground, safe from human-made or natural disaster.

What Can You Do?

Scientists aren't the only people protecting plants. There is also plenty you can do:

- Reduce activities and products that cause pollution. Don't waste electricity, and try walking instead of driving.

- Reuse or recycle as much as you can.

- Share your knowledge of the dangers plants are up against.

- Look for groups that add new plants to creeks, rivers, and other places that have lost plant life.

People need plants. Do what you can to make a difference!

You can grow your own plants in a home, school, or neighborhood garden.

Your Own Tiny Tree

Have you ever seen a bonsai tree? People create these tiny potted trees by carefully trimming the roots and branches as they grow. Bonsais were first grown in China more than 1,000 years ago. Try caring for one yourself.

Materials

Pre-potted bonsai tree, such as a juniper

Water

Bonsai cutting tool

Directions

 1 Visit a garden store to choose your tree. Decide which kind you want. How big will it be? Do you want one that grows outdoors or one that can stay inside the house? Think carefully.

2 Find a place for your tree at home. If you are keeping it indoors, be sure to choose a spot that gets enough sunlight. Water your bonsai regularly and observe how it grows.

3 Over time, its branches will get longer and grow in different directions. Use your cutting tool to prune them into the shape you like.

4 Watch videos and read tips from other bonsai growers. There is a lot to learn about this art form. With practice, you can shape your tree however you like!

Explain It!

Do you think learning how to care for a bonsai tree would teach you skills that are useful in plant-related jobs? Which jobs? If you need help, turn to page 39 for more information.

Approximate number of known plant species: 400,000

Estimated percentage of plant species at risk of extinction: About 20

Number of plant species found in the Amazon rain forest: About 40,000

Percentage of the Amazon rain forest that has been cleared since the 1970s: About 20

Total amount of land used to grow GMO crops around the world: 469,500,225 acres (190 million ha)

Percentage of animal feed that comes from GMO plants: About 88

Did you find the truth?

(T) People need plants to survive.

(F) The first genetically modified plants were produced in 2010.

Resources

Other books in this series:

You can also look at:

Colby, Jennifer. *Growing New Plants*. Ann Arbor, MI: Cherry Lake Publishing, 2015.

Gray, Susan H. *Super Cool Science Experiments: Plants*. Ann Arbor, MI: Cherry Lake Publishing, 2010.

Rattini, Kristin Baird. *Seed to Plant*. Washington, DC: National Geographic, 2014.

Glossary

biodiversity (bye-oh-duh-VUR-suh-tee) the variety of species that live in a single area

fossil fuels (FAH-suhl FYOOLZ) coal, oil, and natural gas, formed from the remains of prehistoric plants and animals

genes (JEENZ) the units through which traits are passed from parent to offspring

hybrid (HYE-brid) a plant or animal that has parents of two different types or species

irrigation (ir-uh-GAY-shuhn) the system that supplies water to crops by human-made means, such as channels or pipes

kingdom (KING-duhm) one of the main groups into which all living things are divided

nomadic (noh-MAD-ik) wandering from place to place instead of living in the same place all the time

nutrients (NOO-tree-uhnts) substances that are needed by animals and plants to stay strong and healthy

photosynthesis (foh-toh-SIN-thuh-sus) a process by which green plants convert light, water, and carbon dioxide into food for themselves and oxygen

species (SPEE-sheez) one of the groups into which organisms are divided; members of the same species can mate and have offspring

Index

Page numbers in **bold** indicate illustrations.

About the Author

Josh Gregory is the author of more than 150 books for young readers. He has written about everything from video games and sports stars to wild animals and U.S. history, but this is his first book about plants. A graduate of the University of Missouri—Columbia, he currently lives in Chicago, Illinois. Each fall, he looks forward to watching the leaves of his neighborhood trees turn from green to beautiful shades of orange, yellow, and red.